Why Does Delvin Bark?

Based on a True Question

Written and illustrated by Corinne Kaz

**Canoe Tree
Press**

Printed in the United States of America
Hardcover ISBN: 978-1-961624-33-7
Paperback ISBN: 978-1-961624-34-4
Ebook ISBN: 978-1-961624-35-1

Canoe Tree Press is a division of DartFrog Books
301 S. McDowell St.
Suite 125-1625
Charlotte, NC 28204
www.DartFrogBooks.com

To Delvin, who was the goodest
(and loudest) boy.
And to Farina, for asking the
question in the first place.

This is Delvin.
Delvin is a dog.

Dogs bark.
Yes.

Does Delvin bark?
Yes, he does.

Why? Tell me!

Delvin barks for a lot of different reasons.

He barks to say "Hello."

He barks to ask if he
can go outside.

He barks to let
us know that
the mail carrier
is on their way.

How does he know?

Oh, he knows.

Those are big barks.
Yes.
Does Delvin make little barks too?
Sometimes.
When?

If he sees a butterfly.

Or a bee.

Or if he is having
a dream.

Or even if he wants to tell us he would like a snack too, please.

Silly Delvin!

But WHY does Delvin bark?

Well, Delvin barks to tell us something,
or to show how he's feeling.
We can use our words to do that, but Delvin uses barks.

I didn't know that
dogs have feelings.

Everyone has feelings.

14

What kind of feelings does Delvin bark about?

Delvin barks when he is
feeling happy, excited, worried,
surprised, hungry, silly, curious,
upset, all kinds of feelings.

Do you ever have these feelings?

Yes!

But if Delvin just barks, how do you know what his feelings are?

I do my best to listen.

Delvin has a lot of feelings.
Oh yes.
I have a lot of feelings too, but I don't
always know their names.

Sometimes it's hard to know
what name to give our feelings.

Sometimes they feel too big!

And sometimes I just need to make
a big noise to let them out.

It's ok to have big feelings!

And it's ok to let them out.

We don't always have to know
what name to give our feelings,
but we can talk about them.

And sometimes, we all just have to make a big noise.

SQUEAL!

CROW

QUACK

THUNDER

YOWL

MEOW

ROAR

CATERWAUL

SING

SNORT

HOOT!

HONK

CLAMOR

BUZZ

BARK

WAIL!

BLEAT!

SQUALL

YAP!

YIP

MEW

YAWP

WHOOP!

YELL

SHRIEK!

SQUAWK!

SCREECH

BELLOW

SNARL

GROWL

SHOUT

TRUMPET

Does Delvin ever bark
to say, "I love you"?
He sure does.

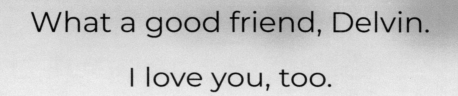

What a good friend, Delvin.

I love you, too.

About the Author

Corinne Kaz is a writer, illustrator and preschool teacher living in Portland, Oregon. She and her partner Will live with their cat Winifred, dogs Ziggy and Blue and six chickens.

103